A Mother's Love

TO MOM

Thanks for listening
Thanks for caring
Thanks for always helping
    in times of need
Thanks for sharing
Thanks Mom,
    for always being there

—Miles M. Hutchinson

Thanks !

Love,

Patty

A Mother's Love

a collection of poems

edited by
Susan Polis Schutz

Blue Mountain Press ™

Boulder, Colorado

Library of Congress Number: 80-67488
ISBN: 0-88396-122-9

Manufactured in the United States of America
First Printing: October, 1980
Second Printing: November, 1981
The following works have previously appeared in Blue Mountain Arts publications:
"Mom, knowing that," by Susan Polis Schutz. Copyright © Continental Publications, 1972. "Since I have a mother," by Susan Polis Schutz. Copyright © Continental Publications, 1973, 1979. "When someone cares," by Susan Polis Schutz. Copyright © Continental Publications, 1974. "Whenever you are happy," by Susan Polis Schutz. Copyright © Continental Publications, 1975, 1979. "Thinking of home" and "A special thought," by Louise Bradford Lowell. Copyright © Continental Publications, 1978 and Copyright © Louise Bradford Lowell, 1978. "Our home," "You have always," "Thinking of you" and "The more I experience," by Andrew Harding Allen. Copyright © Continental Publications, 1979 and Copyright © Andrew Harding Allen, 1979. "To Mom," by Miles M. Hutchinson. Copyright © Continental Publications, 1979 and Copyright © Miles M. Hutchinson, 1979. "A mother represents," by Debra Colin-Cooke. Copyright © Continental Publications, 1979 and Copyright © Debra Colin-Cooke, 1979. "Time cannot change," by Joel Winsome Williams. Copyright © Continental Publications, 1979 and Copyright © Joel Winsome Williams, 1979. "A Mother's Love . . . ," by Virginia Leigh Robbins. Copyright © Continental Publications, 1979 and Copyright © Virginia Leigh Robbins, 1979. "A Mother's Love A special kind of love," by Debra Colin-Cooke. Copyright © Continental Publications, 1980 and Copyright © Debra Colin-Cooke, 1980. All rights reserved.

Thanks to the Blue Mountain Arts creative staff, with special thanks to Douglas Pagels and Faith Hamilton.

ACKNOWLEDGMENTS are on page 64

Blue Mountain Press INC

P.O. Box 4549, Boulder, Colorado 80306

CONTENTS

A Mother's Love

A special kind of love
that's always there when you need it
to comfort and inspire,
yet lets you go your own path.
A sharing heart
filled with patience and forgiveness,
that takes your side
even when wrong.
Nothing can take its place.

—Debra Colin-Cooke

Mom,

Knowing that you are always
here to understand and
accept me helps me get along
in the confused world. If
every person could have
someone just like you, the
world would become a
peaceful garden.

—Susan Polis Schutz

Every thing in nature bespeaks the mother. The sun is the mother of the earth and gives it its nourishment of heat; it never leaves the universe at night until it has put the earth to sleep to the song of the sea and the hymn of the birds and brooks. And this earth is the mother of trees and flowers. It produces them, nurses them, and weans them. The trees and flowers become kind mothers of their great fruits and seeds. And the mother, the prototype of all existence, is the eternal spirit, full of beauty and love.

—Kahlil Gibran

Throughout our lives
as we count our successes
and pat ourselves on the back,
how seldom do we remember
who it was that began it all.
I was very fortunate
in God's decision
that I be given to the woman
I now know as my mother,
for it was she who showed me
how to care, how to love,
how to feel, and how to be free.

—James Bruce Joseph Sievers

Mother

My love for you
is deep and unalterable.
In me, the memory
of your goodness and devotion
will never fade.
I should like to find words
to prove to you
how much I love you,
how my heart is filled
to overflowing with reverence
and gratitude
to you.

—Franz Liszt

Thank You, Mom

Gratitude is the hardest
of all emotions to express.
There is no word capable of
conveying all that one feels.
Until we reach a world
where thoughts can be adequately
expressed in words,
"thank you" will have to do.

—A. P. Gouthey

You have always been there
when I needed you.
Even though we don't always agree
with each other,
our love has always prevailed.
You have taught me kindness
and understanding—
you have given me the ability
to find love in the world.

—Andrew Harding Allen

$\mathcal{A}$ mother represents all the patience and forgiveness that are needed for support throughout one's life.

—Debra Colin-Cooke

Dear Mother,
You will never know
how much I love you . . .
God bless you and keep you,
and my love to you
every minute and always.

—Richard Davis

Forever is the love
that is filled with understanding
Forever is the love
that is true and undemanding
Forever is the love
that can stand the test of time.
Forever I am yours . . .

—Dolly Parton

$\mathcal{I}$ have never met anybody in my life, I think, who loved his mother as much as I love you. I don't believe there ever was anybody who did, quite so much, and quite in so many wonderful ways.

—Edna St. Vincent Millay

To Mother

Whenever you are
happy, I am happy, too
because you
are an important part of me
and my life is
intermingled with your
life.
I love you.

—Susan Polis Schutz

All that I am
or hope to be
I owe to my mother.

—Abraham Lincoln

My dear mother . . .
if you are happy,
I have everything
I can wish for.

—Thomas Moore

The best and most beautiful
things in the world
cannot be seen
or even touched.
They must be felt
with the heart.

—Helen Keller

A Mother's Heart

A mother's heart
holds the fondest memories,
the noblest dreams
for her child.
I am grateful when
I think
of your loving heart,
Mother.
Thanks for letting go
yet clasping me always
to your loving heart.

—Jean Therese Lynch

To Mother

Our HOME is the place where I
first learned to love and where I
first learned to share.

Our HOME is the place where there is a
person who always cares.

Even if I am far away, the memory of
our HOME remains close in my heart.

—Andrew Harding Allen

Many make the household
but only one the home.

—James Russell Lowell

Thinking of home
Thinking of the past
Thinking of tomorrow
Brings me closer to you
You are a special person
who brings lasting joy
into my life

—Louise Bradford Lowell

God could not
be everywhere,
so he created
mothers.

—Jewish proverb

Never, dear Mother
shall I be able to
thank you enough
for helping me
to so much happiness.

—Francis Joseph I

$\mathcal{M}$others are the daughters
of yesterday,
the grandmothers of tomorrow
and the hope of today.

Mothers are the closest to God
one can feel while passing through
this world's great story.

—Edith Schaffer Lederberg

*M*any joys
have touched me through my mother . . .
I've been going through old photographs,
   and pictures I drew in 1st grade,
      my first baby teeth,
         a lock of hair . . .
all the tender, special memories
my Mother saved,
and I smile
and feel warm inside.

Now I'm collecting the treasures
   of my own children . . .
I pray some day they will sort through these,
   and remember . . .
      and smile . . .
         and feel warm inside.

—Sue Mitchell

For Mother

When someone cares
it is easier to speak
it is easier to listen
it is easier to play
it is easier to work

When someone cares
it is easier to laugh

—Susan Polis Schutz

When I think of your loving face,
and of how pleasant it is
to live with you,
of your deep serenity,
your charming tranquility,
I know very well that
I shall never love anyone
as much as you.

—Gustave Flaubert

I search among the plain
  and lovely words
To find what the one word
  "Mother" means . . .

"Mother"—a word that holds
  the tender spell
Of all the dear essential
  things of earth;
A home, clean sunlit rooms,
  and the good smell
Of bread; a table spread;
  a glowing hearth.
And love beyond
  the dream of anyone . . .
I search for words for her . . .
  and there are none.

                        —Grace Noll Crowell

Mothers

God made mothers more special than anyone else. He made them the bearers of life and in so doing, knew they had to be more exceptional than the rest of us. He made them the cornerstone of the home, the foundation of the family, the backbone of society, the ideal of all that is best with the human race. They are the guardians of decency, the preservers of peace, the upholders of truth, the protectors of morality, the symbol of virtue, an inspiration to all that is noble and good in life, and love knows no greater representative than that of a mother's love. Upon our earth, no title is more revered and no sound more beautiful or sweeter heard than the tender loving word—mother.

—Daniel Haughian

Mother is the name
for God
in the lips and hearts
of little children.

—William Makepeace Thackeray

What a wonderful thing
  is a mother!
Other folks can love you,
  but only your mother understands;
She works for you—
  looks after you—
Loves you, forgives you . . .

—Baroness von Hutton

She is just an extraordinary
mother and a gentle person.
I depended on her for everything . . .
I watched her become
a strong person,
and that had an enormous
influence on me.

—Rosalynn Carter

It seems God moves about her
more freely than He does most people,
and that the soul of Mother
is in some way so familiar
with His presence that
she doesn't think to title
their relationship.

—Joan Baez

Mom

The hardest job has gone to you
To you who means the most to me
You've always been there
   to pick me up
   and guide me
There to scream and yell
   or to sit and listen
You've shared my happiness
   my love
   my sickness
   and health

You've felt pride
   and disappointment

Most of all,
   you've loved me
   and always will

—Donna Elker

Time cannot change . . .
 a warm sunrise in the
  morning
 children playing in the fields
 a sea gull soaring in the sky
 the honest curiosity of a child
Time cannot change
 the kindness and
  understanding of
 a Mother's love

—Joel Winsome Williams

The more I experience life
   the more I realize
That a mother as great as you
   is really very rare.

—Andrew Harding Allen

If she hadn't been there to
support and encourage me, I
might not have grown up to
be the confident person I am.

—Marlo Thomas

A Mother's Love . . .

Love that is always there
    when you need it
Love that knows all
    your needs
Love that comforts when
    you feel sad
Love that is generous
    and patient
Love that is more understanding
    with every passing year

—Virginia Leigh Robbins

I must tell you how much
I love you; that with each day
I learn to extol your love
and your worth more—
and that when I look back
over my life, I can find nothing
in your treatment of me
that I would alter.

I believe, most beloved mother,
that the improvement of the world
can only arise when mothers
like you are increased
thousands of times
and have more children.

—Louis D. Brandeis

TIME FOR MOTHER

1. Take time to give mother
   Due honor and praise;
   For all of her patience
   Through our childhood days.
   In all of her troubles
   She looked to the Lord;
   And taught all her children
   To trust in His Word.

2. Take time to thank mother
   For all she has done;
   In telling her children
   Of God's only Son.
   She told you how Jesus
   Once died on the tree;
   To purchase salvation
   For you and for me.

3. Thank God for a mother
   Who feareth the Lord;
   Who teaches her children
   To honor His Word.
   Who taught you to reverence
   And love the Lord's Day;
   Who prays for her children
   Lest they go astray.

4. Many of our mothers
   Aren't with us today;
   They're now up in heaven
   All tears wiped away.
   But someday we'll meet them
   Reunion complete;
   And worship with mother
   Down at Jesus' feet.

TEXT - Anna Mary Beach
MUSIC - George C. Stebbins

A special thought
for you, Mom

We all need
a person to understand
Someone to share our
thoughts with
and always be around
in time of need
We all need
a person like you

—Louise Bradford Lowell

$\mathcal{I}$ hope, my own dear mother,
that you are as well
and happy at home
as my heart wishes you to be.

—Thomas Moore

$\mathcal{I}$ keep thinking
about you
every few minutes
all day.

—Walt Whitman

*M*y dear Mother, the growth
of a lifetime is not cut down by
absence . . . let me tell you as
earnestly and gladly as I can,
that I never loved you so
devotedly as I do this
moment. That every day on
which I have delayed to write,
you have been before
my eyes . . .

That in my happiest hours,
my happiness has been
incomplete without you.

—Edmund Clarence Stedman

Of your love I am always so sure
that it needed no such kind words
as you write to assure me
of my precious possession of it.
But it is good to feel it come
so near me.

—Lincoln Steffens

Mother

She showed me how to love
   when I thought I knew how
She was there to kiss away
   the tears when I was hurt
She was there to let me try my wings
   and help the hurt go away
   when things didn't go the way
   I had planned
She was there with her love
   to make me feel special
She was there with
   her knowledge and wisdom
   when I faced a new experience
I pray that when I am lucky enough
   to become a mother, I will be
   as kind and as loving as mine

—Donna Wayland

To Mom

What greater thing is there
for two human souls
than to feel that they are
joined for life—
to strengthen each other
in all labor,
to rest on each other
in all sorrow,
to minister to each other
in all pain,
and to be with each other
in silent unspeakable memories . . .

—George Eliot

Thinking of you,
Mother

The happiness that families share
is the greatest joy in the world.
The knowledge that there is always someone
who cares is a treasure nothing can match.
The love of a family
makes life beautiful.

—Andrew Harding Allen

Mother darling,

𝕴t is wonderful to meet
and talk over everything
and share and laugh
and understand each other's situations
as no one else can.

—Anne Morrow Lindbergh

Dear Mother

You know that nothing
can ever change
what we have always been
and always will be
to each other.

—Franklin Delano Roosevelt

total filling and flooding
of body and heart
in the silence of the mother's embrace
transcending all other forms of feeling
touching the higher realms
of comfort . . . safety . . . surrender
floating gently in the ethers
of the universal womb
simple and complete knowing
you have been brought to . . .
and . . . now . . . are held closely within
the soft and constant bosom
of mother love

—diane westlake

For all you have done
   for the gifts you have given
For the love you have shown
   in the life we are living

I thank you
with the whole of my heart.

—Andrew Tawney

To my Mother:
My help and my inspiration,
the one who has had
faith in me always
and who has stood by me
in brightest day and darkest night.
To my only sweetheart,
my Mother.

—Octavus Roy Cohen

$\mathcal{M}$y sentiments remain the same . . . the feeling of thanks for that grand love of yours towards your child, which you displayed so warmly and so tenderly.

—Richard Wagner

$\mathcal{M}$y ever-loved Mother,
I salute you with my affection
once more, and thank you
for bringing me into this world,
and for all your unwearied
care over me there.
May God reward you for it—
as assuredly He will
and does.

—Thomas Carlyle

Since I have a mother
whose many interests
keep her excited and occupied

Since I have a mother
who interacts with so many people
that she has a real feeling for
the world

Since I have a mother
who always is strong
through any period of suffering

Since I have a mother
who is a complete person
I always have a model
to look up to
and that makes it easier
for me to develop into
an independent person
Thanks, Mom

—Susan Polis Schutz

ACKNOWLEDGMENTS

We gratefully acknowledge the permission granted by the following authors, publishers and authors' representatives to reprint poems and excerpts from their publications.

Harcourt Brace Jovanovich, Inc. for "Mother darling," by Anne Morrow Lindbergh. From the book THE FLOWER AND THE NETTLE. Copyright © 1976 by Anne Morrow Lindbergh. All rights reserved. Reprinted by permission.

Donna Wayland for "Mother." Copyright © Donna Wayland, 1978. All rights reserved. Reprinted by permission.

The Viking Press, Inc. for "I must tell you how much," by Louis D. Brandeis. From the book BRANDEIS: A FREE MAN'S LIFE, by Alpheus Thomas Mason. Copyright © 1946 by Alpheus Thomas Mason; reprinted by permission of the publisher, The Viking Press, Inc., N.Y.

Redbook for "If she hadn't been there," by Marlo Thomas. From the February, 1977 issue of Redbook. All rights reserved. Reprinted by permission.

Donna Elker for "Mom." Copyright © Donna Elker, 1978. All rights reserved. Reprinted by permission.

Chandos Productions for "It seems God moves about her," by Joan Baez. From the book DAYBREAK, by Joan Baez. Copyright © 1966, 1968 by Joan Baez. All rights reserved. Reprinted by permission.

McCall Publishing Company for "She is just," by Rosalynn Carter. From the April, 1977 issue of McCall's. All rights reserved. Reprinted by permission.

Daniel Haughian for "Mothers." Copyright © Daniel Haughian, 1979. All rights reserved. Reprinted by permission.

Harper & Row, Publishers, Inc. for "I search among the plain," by Grace Noll Crowell. Fr m the book LIGHT OF THE YEARS by Grace Noll Crowell. Copyright 1936 by Harper & Row, Publishers, Inc.; renewed 1964 by Grace Noll Crowell. All rights reserved. Reprinted by permission.

Velvet Apple Music for "Forever is the love," by Dolly Parton. From the song SAY FOREVER YOU'LL BE MINE, by Dolly Parton. Copyright © 1971 by Owepar Publishing Co. All rights reserved. Reprinted by permission.

John Schaffner for "I have never met," by Edna St. Vincent Millay. From the book LETTERS OF EDNA ST. VINCENT MILLAY, edited by Allan Ross Macdougall. Published by Harper and Brothers, Copyright © 1952 by Norma Millay Ellis. Copyright © 1952 by Allan Ross Macdougall. All rights reserved. Reprinted by permission.

Lyle Stuart, Inc. for "Every thing in nature," by Kahlil Gibran. From the book A THIRD TREASURY OF KAHLIL GIBRAN edited by Andrew Dib Sherfan. Copyright © 1975, 1973, 1966, 1965 by Philosophical Library, Inc. All rights reserved. Reprinted by permission.

Edith Schaffer Lederberg for "Mothers are the daughters," by Edith Schaffer Lederberg. Copyright © 1979 by Edith Schaffer Lederberg. All rights reserved. Reprinted by permission.

Sue Mitchell for "Many joys," by Sue Mitchell. Copyright © 1980 by Sue Mitchell. All rights reserved. Reprinted by permission.

Jean Therese Lynch for "A Mother's Heart," by Jean Therese Lynch. Copyright © 1980 by Jean Therese Lynch. All rights reserved. Reprinted by permission.

Starboard Publishing Company for "Throughout our lives," by James Bruce Joseph Sievers. Copyright © 1976 by Starboard Publishing Company. All rights reserved. Reprinted by permission.

Diane Westlake for "total filling and flooding," by diane westlake. Copyright © Diane Westlake, 1980. All rights reserved. Reprinted by permission.

If any error or omission has occurred, it is completely inadvertent, and we would like to correct it in future editions provided that written notification is made to the publisher: BLUE MOUNTAIN PRESS, INC., P.O. Box 4549, Boulder, Colorado 80306.